Perspectives
Caught on Camera
The Power of Photography

Series Consultant: Linda Hoyt

Flying Start
to Literacy®

T0360034

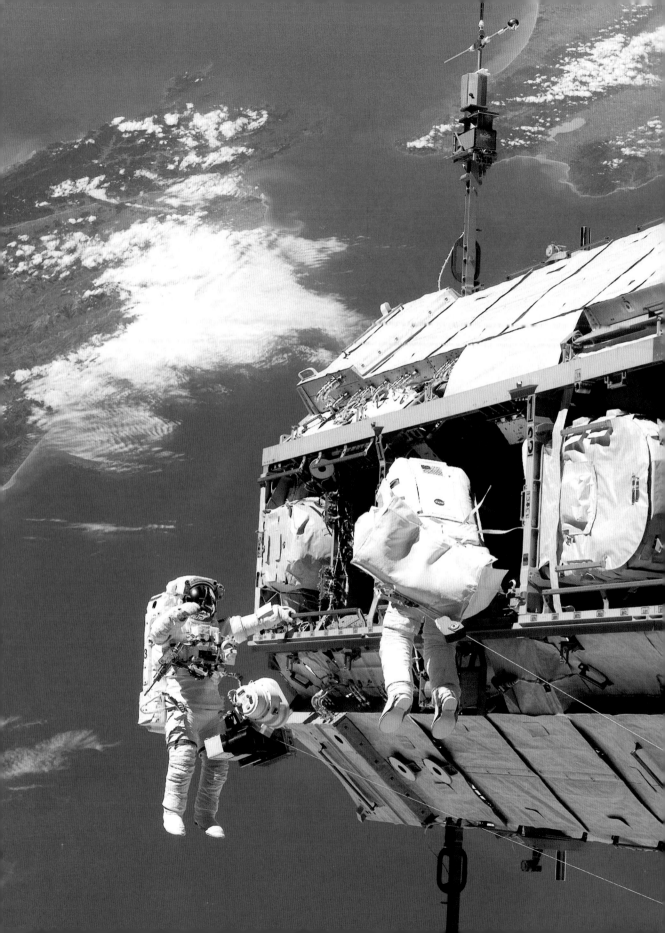

Contents

Images are powerful. What is the responsibility of the photographer?

Photographs can make us want to buy things, go places or feel emotions. They can teach us things. Millions of images are uploaded to social media every day. Once an image is made public on social media, it may be impossible to remove.

Why are we so obsessed with taking photographs and sharing them? How careful should you be posting photos on social media?

The power of pictures

Photos have the power to direct people's attention to particular events in the world. When photos are seen by millions of people worldwide, they can be a signal for change or a call to action. Sometimes photos can be used to persuade us to a particular point of view.

These photos, some from the past and some very recent, are recognised around the world. Why are these photographs so compelling? Can you imagine why each photographer took that particular picture?

Last Polar Bear:
This photograph was taken in the Arctic Circle.

Migrant Mother: This photograph was taken in California, USA, in 1936 during the Great Depression.

Fastest Man in the World: Usain Bolt competing in the Men's 100 metre semifinal during the Olympic Games, 14 August 2016 in Rio de Janeiro, Brazil.

Moon Landing: Astronaut Edwin "Buzz" Aldrin stands beside the US flag after it was unfurled on the moon surface in 1969.

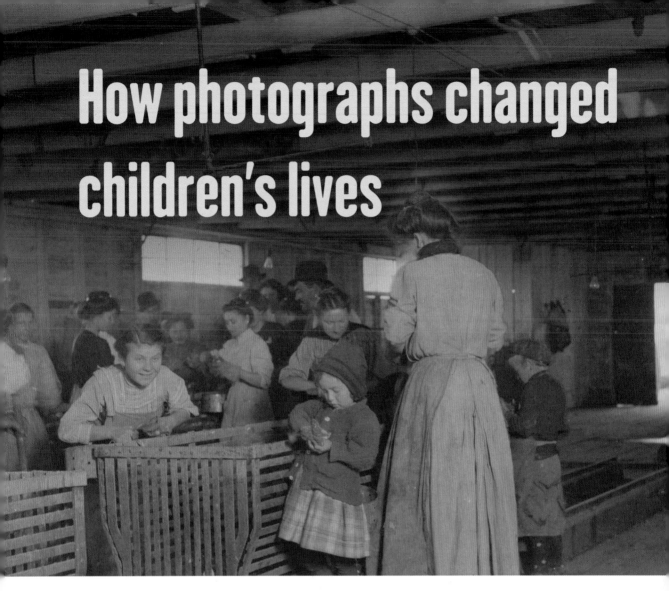

How photographs changed children's lives

In her article about the photographer Lewis Hine, journalist Marcia Amidon Lusted reminds us of a time when photography became a powerful tool for telling stories. Lewis Hine's photographs of children in the workplace in the United States in the early 20th century helped change the way people thought about working children and led to changes in the law that would make it harder to exploit children.

If Lewis Hine was alive today, what photographs do you think he would be taking?

For many of the "kids at work" in the 1800s and early 1900s, work was difficult and dangerous. Many Americans began demanding an end to child labour. They fought for the rights of children to have a childhood.

One of these people was a New York City schoolteacher and photographer named Lewis Hine. He quit his teaching job and became an investigative photographer for the National Child Labor Committee, a group started in 1904 to work for child labour reforms.

Two young girls working in a hosiery mill in Tennessee, USA, 1910.

"I am sure I am right in my choice of work," Hine told a friend. "My child labour photos have already set the authorities to work to see if such things can be possible."

Hine's photographs are still powerful today. Through them, you can see the faces of children just like you but who spent their lives working in often terrible conditions. Partly because of the work of Lewis Hine, you don't have to do what these children did.

Breaker boys worked underground in coal mines, picking slate out from the coal.

Addie Card, aged 12, worked as a spinner in a cotton mill in 1910.

Kids using social media

Opening a social media account is generally restricted to people aged 13 and above. But the number of children aged 13 and under who have social media accounts is definitely on the rise. In this article, 14-year-old Ruth Quinn argues social media can affect children in positive *and* negative ways.

Should children under the age of 13 use social media? What's your opinion?

Social media is a quick and easy way to communicate. If it wasn't for apps like Snapchat and Instagram, I wouldn't have stayed in touch with some of my friends and relatives who live far away. Looking through my home feed on Instagram or searching on YouTube is a great way to discover new things and gain new skills.

Personally, I like to think of my Instagram like a photo album or picture chronicle. My Instagram is a place to store memories. It shows a journey of some of the most significant – mostly good – moments of my life. Things like holidays, sporting achievements and the everyday events that are more for me than anyone else.

But some kids use social media to gain popularity. If a post doesn't get the desired number of likes in a certain period of time, then it gets deleted. Some sites are places to judge and be judged, but if you get negative comments you can feel pretty bad about yourself. Often, there is pressure to be perfect, to have the ultimate life and go to the most picturesque places. This pressure can be immensely stressful.

It is also easy to share too much on social media. Once you post a photo or send a message, it could be circulating the web forever. You never really know who is seeing what, so making sure you don't share too much is a vital aspect of owning any social media account. Some underage users send images and messages that they will later regret.

One more thing: it is very easy to become addicted to social media because you never want to miss anything. You feel the need to constantly check your device. This can make you disconnected from the world around you, and you might start treating people badly.

Getting the shot

Author Mary-Anne Creasy spoke to Brisbane-based photographer Mike Curtain about the impact photographic drones are having on his profession. This raises the question of privacy.

What's your opinion? How important is your privacy to you?

Mike Curtain

**Drones are being used a lot in the photography industry.
What are they mainly being used for, and why?**

*Sometimes I need to photograph something from a height. A client might
want to show land for future housing developments, or I might take a photo
for a tourism business. I have also had to take an aerial photograph of
a car driving on a road for an advertisement.*

*In the past, we had to use helicopters or cranes to get the height for these
types of shots. But helicopters are large, noisy, and considering I have to
hang out the side to take the photos, a bit dangerous. There are strict safety
rules as to how low a helicopter can fly and how close one can fly to an object
like a building or mountain. Helicopters are expensive to hire and to fly.*

*Cranes are the same – they are expensive. You can't use them safely on
a slope or on unstable ground. There are problems if they are near other
structures, and they can't move quickly or easily.*

*But now I can use a drone,
which is small, quite cheap and,
of course, much safer. They
can fly close to buildings and
other objects; they can fly low;
and there are not as many rules
or restrictions when operating
them as there are when using a
helicopter or a crane. I can fly
a drone myself so it's quicker to
get the shots I need.*

Do you think people should be concerned about their privacy now there are drones being used in photography?

Drones have allowed photographers to easily and cheaply take photos and videos from elevated points of view. However, because drones are so new, there are not many laws in place regarding privacy.

I think there is a responsibility for the drone operator to be sensitive to other people's concerns about privacy. Drone operators are only encouraged to respect people's privacy, but like ordinary photography, it's still not against the law to take photos of people, with or without a drone.

When I'm out in public taking photos, people can see it's me taking the photos. They can ask me questions about what I'm using the photos for and why I'm taking them. But if a drone is flying around with no operator in sight, who knows who owns it or what it's doing?

A drone can photograph what happens in people's backyards.

Although I'm excited about the advantages a drone will give me as a photographer, as an ordinary person I would be concerned if there was a drone hovering above my backyard. I think because it's new technology, it may take a while for privacy concerns to be taken seriously.

I personally think that whether a drone is being flown for recreational or professional use, all operators should have to be licensed and pass a test – as you do to have a driver's licence – so that drone operators understand their responsibilities.

Friends told me that they were having a picnic at a park, enjoying the peace and quiet, when someone arrived and started flying a noisy drone around. You can imagine how annoying that would be, knowing there's nothing you can do except hope the battery runs out soon!

Say it with photos

Sharing photos on social media is an instant way to send a message to many people. Kathryn Hulick joined Instagram while working on this article. She says real-time conversations are being replaced with photo streams on social media sites. The first photo she posted was of her new puppy.

Do you think the stories that are told on social media sites accurately reflect people's lives?

Click, tap, share!

With a swipe of your finger across the screen of a smartphone, the entire world can now see the dancing trick you just taught your dog. The first comment comes in a few moments later: "So cute!!!" Sharing a photo from your phone through social media is faster, easier and much more fun than waiting until school tomorrow and using words to tell your friends about what happened.

The number of photos we take and share is growing astronomically as the technology becomes easier to use and more accessible to everyone. Mobile photography and social media mean you can share pictures and talk about your experience as it happens, in real time.

"Like" me!

Sharing and looking at photos is the most popular thing to do on social networking sites. You're twice as likely to "like" a photo compared to a text comment. Teens aged 13 to 17 report that they spend more than nine hours a week using social networking sites. Photo activities such as sharing, liking and commenting make up about 30 per cent of that time, according to a study by InfoTrends. Associate Director Alan Bullock says, "Facebook has grown like crazy because they embraced photo sharing early on and made it a core feature of their site."

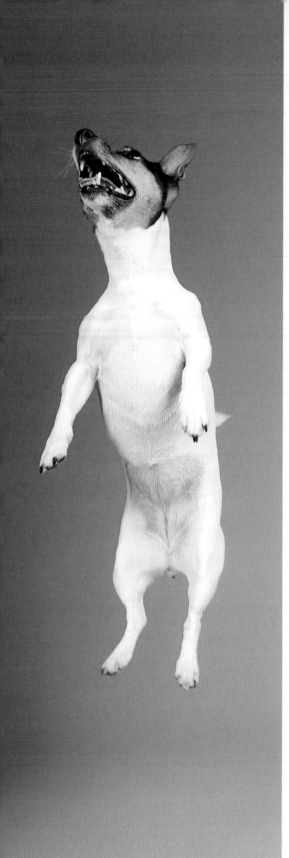

Going mobile

When your dog starts dancing, do you reach for your digital camera, knowing that you'll have to sit down and extract the photo in order to share it, or do you reach for your phone? I bet the phone wins out.

"Particularly among younger social network users, mobile devices like smartphones and tablets are being used to capture more and more photos and videos," says Bullock. "Those users will demand easy access and simple uploading, viewing and sharing, regardless of the device being used."

Telling stories

Many of the photos we take now don't get sorted or stored to look at later. "Photography now is much more part of an ongoing story – almost like speaking visually," says Jesse Chan-Norris, a New York-based photographer. "Mobile photography is not really meant to be captured and archived."

Would it bother you if you never again got to see the photos you and your friends shared this week? It could happen. If you only keep your photos on your phone, and then one day you drop it in a puddle, you may not be able to easily go back, find and save the pictures you've shared on social networks.

This is because photos uploaded to Facebook or Instagram get shrunk down to a smaller size and resolution. If you delete the original picture or don't back it up anywhere, you may never have a big enough version to print. But maybe that's not really a problem. You don't expect to save every conversation you've ever had, right? In many ways, social photos are just another way to talk to each other – they are single images with much longer stories to tell.

What is your opinion?: How to write a persuasive argument

1. State your opinion

Think about the issues related to your topic. What is your opinion?

2. Research

Research the information you need to support your opinion.

Related PERSPECTIVES book   Internet   Other sources

3. Make a plan

Introduction
How will you "hook" the reader?
State your opinion.

List reasons to support your opinion.
What persuasive devices will you use?

Reason 1
Support your reason
with evidence and details.

Reason 2
Support your reason
with evidence and details.

Reason 3
Support your reason
with evidence and details.

Conclusion
Restate your opinion. Leave your reader with a strong message.

4. Publish

Publish your persuasive argument.
Use visuals to reinforce your opinion.

© 2018 EC Licensing Pty Ltd.